CONTENTS

Preface   Hooked on shells

Shell lady.............

HOOKED ON SHELLS.

To have one great love affair in a lifetime is breathtaking but to have more than one is akin to finding the pot of gold at the end of the rainbow.

As resident housekeeper at A la Ronde I am in the happy situation of being employed in the safekeeping and conservation of the house and its contents.

I will never forget the day, back in February of 1991 that I turned into the driveway from Summer Lane and saw A la Ronde for the first time. It was love at first sight, the quirky red diamond windows, the honey-pot shape, the way it nestled into the meadow and as I drew nearer the great air of dilapidation which tugged at my heart strings. Although I had never been to the house or even heard of its whereabouts before, I felt as if I had come home. The discovery of the Shell Gallery, though in a parlous state was joyous, with even more wonders of shellwork around the house than I could have imagined.

My part in looking after all of these, includes the conservation and repair of the shell gallery and the responsibility for the shell collections at A la Ronde, a subject very close to my heart as shells have always been of special interest to me.

Part of my remit was to write a few notes about sea shells………………. a sentence or two……………., however, my passion for shells has taken over, hence this little book.

Never intended to be scholarly or scientific, these jottings are purely for interest and enjoyment and if they intrigue enough for you to delve further, I can thoroughly recommend the pastime. Myself?.......... I am a shell addict!

The Slater Collection A la Ronde

Have you ever lifted a large shell to your ear and listened......? If so, you will know that it is possible to hear the sea.

"Less than a God they thought there could not dwell,
Within the hollow of that shell
That spoke so sweetly."
(Dryden)

THE SEA SHELL

Aesthetically and functionally formed the seashell is the hard outer case of a soft bodied mollusc, purpose built to house and defend its occupant from the rigors of the sea. Veritable cities of self-built single dwellings exist therein, shaped and coloured to blend with surroundings, as protection against predators.

Naturally produced from the mantle or body of the resident mollusc are the building materials. The lower body which protrudes from the shell manufactures conchiolin for the outside wall and calcium carbonate for the middle section. The grand interior, which is emitted from the whole mantle, is the most exquisite. Laid down in thin sheets, aragonite, the beautiful opalescence known as "Mother-of-Pearl" or nacre, enhances the interior. These three layers complete the main structure; no cement

The Great Green Turban Shell.
Highly polished to reveal the nacreous Aragonite interior (the Hypostracum), the white circle shows the central layer (the Ostracum), topped with the green outer layer of conchiolin (The Periostracum.)
These three layers combine to form
THE SHELL.

mixers or building sites necessary, just the sheer ingenuity of Mother Nature.

As the inhabitant of the shell grows these secretions continue so that the "house" is never too small. From birth to death the shell and mollusc grow together making it possible to tell the age by marks of growth, similar to tree rings. Shell exteriors range from granular, plain, and fairly colourless to smooth, vibrant and exotic, depending on habitat and temperature.

Warmth, as in the plant and animal kingdom, produces the most spectacularly coloured shells. The richest shell neighbourhood is The Indo-Pacific Province which encompasses The Red Sea, the Tropical Northern half of Australia, The Hawaiian Chain and The Philippines.

The English Channel, a pretty cold neighbourhood in comparison, deposits a very large selection of shells on our shores. They cannot compete with the colours of sunnier climes, but they never disappoint in abundance and variety. Each one is a designer home in its own right.

The death of a home owner renders the "shell house" as a vacant possession, highly advantageous to a passing Hermit crab seeking a larger dwelling; but mainly it is left to the mercy of the sea. The pull and push of strong tides and currents moves the shell hither and thither buffeting and grinding it until it becomes so fragmented it settles on the sea bed to form part of the sandy bottom.

A large number are thrown up, some slightly damaged, others in broken bits, but best of all, some still intact.

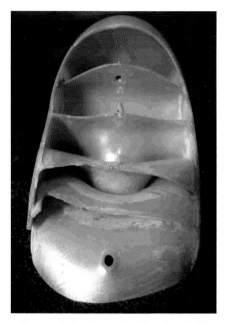

Exposed chambers of a Nautilus shell

Spiral interior of a Common Whelk

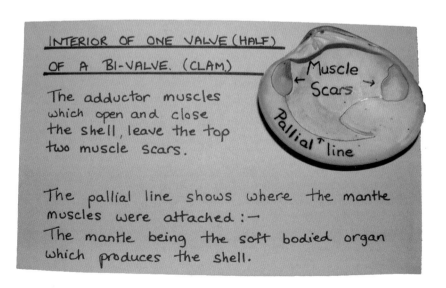

INTERIOR OF ONE VALVE (HALF)

OF A BI-VALVE. (CLAM.)

The adductor muscles which open and close the shell, leave the top two muscle scars.

Muscle Scars

Pallial line

The pallial line shows where the mantle muscles were attached :—
The mantle being the soft bodied organ which produces the shell.

All have their own points of interest. The broken bits do not always resemble their original form, as the continual movement of the sea smoothes the rough edges and reshapes them. It is fun to try and guess what they once were.

Curiosity about others' homes renders the partially damaged shell most interesting as it provides a good peek at the inside. The "Mother-of-Pearl" lining is not always as polished and perfect as we see in the best shell collections but has promise. Some reveal remains of beautiful spiral columns resembling little staircases, while others expose indentations or muscle scars which show how the mollusc was secured. Small and perfect hinges become visible for the first time.

Comparing a complete shell with a damaged one of a like specimen is very thought provoking, so simple yet so complex.

It is said that no house is complete without a door. In the great estates of sea shells, this additional feature is known

as the operculum. Attached to the tail of the owner this precisely shaped disc of a horny, limy substance seals the entrance when the animal withdraws, providing perfect security.

Operculum

Unlike shells the operculum is seldom to be found upon British shores as it is normally lost at sea with the mollusc. However, more sophisticated examples are washed up in the tropics.

South African Turban shell & its pustulated operculum

COLLECTING

The phylum mollusca is one of the major branches of the animal kingdom, therefore with over one hundred thousand living forms, the collector is spoilt for choice.

However amateur or professional the collection there is always the same buzz of excitement at a "new find" or acquisition.

Robert Louis Stevenson wrote *"It is perhaps a more fortunate destiny to have a taste for collecting shells than to be born a millionaire"*.

Those lucky enough to live near the sea have the great advantage of regularly seeking out beached shells, an occupation particularly rewarding after a bad storm. However, to aid conservation, only empty shells should be gathered in order to maintain the balance of nature.

A freshly washed sandy shore might appear to be totally uninhabited (apart from the gulls) but nothing could be further from the truth; beneath the sand dwells a host of burrowers, the majority on our British shores being bivalves (two parts or valves), Cockles, Tellins, Wedge, Venus and

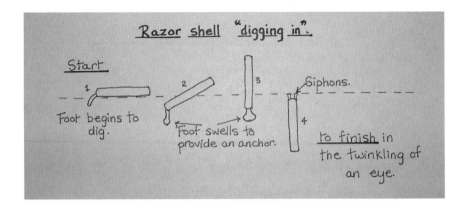

Razor shell "digging in".

Start

1 Foot begins to dig.

2 Foot swells to provide an anchor.

3

4 Siphons. To finish in the twinkling of an eye.

Razor shells are just a few. Each has a muscular foot which is pushed into the sediment and by a series of muscular contractions both shell and occupant are swiftly drawn down into the sand, disappearing out of harms way. The Common Piddock favours soft rock such as clay or limestone into which it bores a burrow by using its flattened foot in conjunction with the rasp-like forepart of its shell. Comfortably ensconced, it remains within the burrow, extending its siphon to feed. The shells, which resemble small Angel's wings, are found fairly frequently around our shores.

At low tide on the lower shore, the small rock pools and drifts of shingle heaped against the rocks make a good search area for Edible Winkles, Top shells, Dog Whelk, Common Whelks, and Sting Winkles.

Dog Whelk
Striated Venus
Common Limpet
Painted Top
Flat Winkles
Blue-rayed Limpets
Banded Wedge   Edible winkle   Sting winkle   Thin Tellin

Common Northern Buccinum (Whelk)

Common European Cockle

Common Blue Mussel

European Piddock

European Razor Clam

Our old friend the Mussel moors itself by means of byssus threads, silky threads discharged from a gland on the hinder part of its foot, which harden in the water as the foot is withdrawn. This glue-like matter, attaches itself to the very smoothest surface, providing an anchor, so strong, that a local legend says that the town authorities in Bideford, (North Devon) forbade the removal of mussels from the bridge piers as they believed that the binding powers of the byssus, instead of mortar, bonded the stones of the bridge together.

Another "strong man", the limpet, grazes on the rocks and may travel some distance in the course of feeding, but always returns to its original spot, whereupon, it seals itself so firmly to the rock surface, it is able to withstand a pull

Mussel beds at Dawlish, Devon

of about forty kilos. An investigation of the seaweed often proves useful and may turn up a cheery yellow, orange or brown Flat Winkle, easy to spot amongst the dark green wrack. Good fortune may also reveal The Blue Rayed Limpet which lives and feeds on Laminaria (Oar-weed). Young specimens are usually found on the fronds whereas the more mature are attached to the holdfasts (roots).

Equipped with a greater knowledge of habitat, collecting becomes more specific, especially necessary when particular shells are sought.

Exchanging and purchasing are alternative options for swelling the collection, but nothing can compare with the satisfaction and excitement of finding "something special" through your own endeavours. It is also true that your "something special" does not always smell that way when unpacked at home.

Exmouth Beach

An overnight soak in dilute bleach followed by a cold water rinse restores all to favour.

Thorough drying is important.

Spread on thick paper towels and dry naturally at room temperature.

Before the treasure trove is tucked away, some data must be recorded.

Select some good quality paper cut into labels, a black marker pen and something with which to measure.

1. Give the shell a catalogue number.

2. Measure it lengthways and widthways for the record.

3. Write the date and exact location of the find and by whom

4. If possible the name of the specimen.

Bivalvia/1	7cmx3cm	04.10.2003. Exmouth beach. MJA.	Mytilus edulis. L. 1758 Common Blue Mussel

Identification is not always easy, but once cleaned and recorded the shell names can be researched at leisure.

The best methods for storage are plastic boxes with removable lids or glass tubes plugged with cotton wool, making sure the relevant label accompanies the correct shell and ideally, kept in a steel cabinet with shallow display drawers, beneficial for protection against light and humidity.

PHYLUM MOLLUSCA:- A major primary division of the animal kingdom made up of classes of soft-bodied, un-segmented animals usually having a hard shell.

classes
MONOPLACOPHORA-   Primitive Limpet- like shells.

Monoplacophora - segmented limpets or gastroverms.
A deep-sea, primitive group, until fairly recently known from fossils.
Limpet shape.

POLYPLACOPHORA-   Chitons.

Polyplacophora.

Chiton

GASTROPODA-   Snails and Slugs.

Gastropoda . Snail.

SCAPHOPODA-   Tusk shells

Scaphopoda.

Tusk shell.

BIVALVIA- Bi-valves (Clams, Mussels and Oysters)

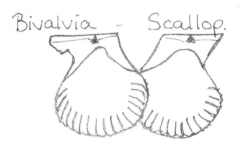

Bivalvia - Scallop.

CEPHALOPODA- Squids, Octopuses and Chambered Nautilus.

Cephalopoda.

Chambered Nautilus.

HIDDEN DANGER

Although no longer vulnerable to predators, an empty shell is still prey to other danger. Stealthier than the crunch of a foot and invisible "to boot" –Bynes disease, called a disease but in reality a chemical reaction.

The visible signs are scarring and the appearance of white powder or crystals accompanied by a strong smell of vinegar (acetic acid).

"The Corrosion of Shells in Cabinets", published by Loftus St George Byne in 1899, outlined a problem which destroyed shell collections. His paper identified a breakdown in the structure of shells which he believed was due to bacterial attack. Later research dismissed this theory but his name is still attributed to the so-called disease.

Almost a century later, in 1985, a more detailed paper was produced by N. H. Tennent and T. Baird who concentrated their studies on the storage of shells in Oak cabinets kept in the temperate climate of North Western Europe. Their findings showed that most of the efflorescence (surface salt crystallization) was caused by volatile acetic and formic acids generated by the Oak cabinets in which shells were stored.

The vapours containing acetic and formic acid, which attack the shell, are a product of the natural decay of cellulose found in wood and associated materials, Oak being one of the worst offenders.

At room temperature they float in the air and attack the calcium carbonate within the shell turning it into calcium acetate. These salts are hygroscopic, which means they attract water, so in highly humid conditions the damage is quickly escalated.

Within an unventilated wooden cabinet displaying shells in cardboard trays or boxes, the acid emissions, which readily dissolve in water, do so in the damp atmosphere turning water vapour into acid vapour; this, combined with the hygroscopic ability of already formed salt crystals means a large amount of acid is absorbed by the shells causing a deadly self-perpetuating cycle.

Badly affected areas are impossible to restore but an attempt to halt the reaction can be made by soaking in strong alcohol for a day and drying thoroughly, alternatively, soaking in fresh water for up to 48 hours, before rinsing under running water whilst scrubbing with a toothbrush and again drying thoroughly. A light application of mineral oil is said to give the shell a little protection but prevention, rather than cure, is without doubt the best method. ☺ Good ventilation, combined with the appropriate storage and temperature conditions will reward the collector.

Treated shells should not be returned to the same environment before conditions inside the cabinet have been rectified.

☺see COLLECTING

NOTHING NEW

Shells have sustained their interest over the centuries

Ammonite impression, Rocks at Charmouth

from the first known appearance as fossils over 500 million years ago. Evolution to our delight has continued to create an enormous increase in ☺genera and species. Throughout this long period of time many great natural historians studied and wrote the first early findings and conchological works based on their travels and the shells they collected. The Greek philosopher Aristotle (384 – 322 BC) was also an exceptional natural historian to whom we attribute the word "mollusca" or "soft-bodied". Pliny the Elder (23 – 79AD), author of Historia Naturalis, made his contribution as a writer and witty raconteur. One of the first to publish, much later in 1616, was Fabius Columna, a Neopolitan physician, his book provided drawings and etchings in his own hand, enabling other collectors to make comparisons. Martin Lister, an English physician followed suit with The Historia Conchyliorum in 1685. The hundreds of illustrations within its pages must have caused a stir amongst conchologists raising expectations for their own collections.

☺ classes having common characteristics.

Gaius Julius Caesar Germanicus (12 – 41AD) otherwise known as the megalomaniac Caligula, suffered from delusions. His sudden interest in shells may have been just another delusion, but was more likely to have been a desire to impress. He became the third Roman Emperor in AD 39 and a year later led a mysterious expedition against Britain. He marched his troops to France and halted them on the beaches of Gaul. His men waited for "Battle Orders" but instead he ordered them, "Gather Seashells!" A large bounty was promised to the soldiers who could fill their tunics and helmets to the brim with "plunder from the sea". Carts full of shells were paraded through the streets on his return home, more the spoils of a battle against Neptune, than a confrontation with the enemy.

More reasonably, the ancient Greeks used great numbers of shells for the ballot box (the people of Athens recorded their votes on public occasions by marks upon a shell).

" He whom ungrateful Athens would expel,
At all times just, but when he signed the shell"

Pope.

Centuries after this tale, a story closer to home is that of "The Prince of shell collectors", Hugh Cuming (1791 – 1865) born on Valentines Day in the village of Washbrook near Kingsbridge, South Devon. A sail-maker by trade who became so successful in business that he was able to retire at a comparatively young age and achieve his ambition to amass the greatest shell collection ever! To do this and further his "collecting horizons", he built his own yacht, The Discoverer, and set off on three fruitful expeditions. He sailed around the Polynesian Islands, the West Coast of South America and The Philippines. The last proved to be the most exciting when he found the first two live specimens of the "Glory of the Sea" (*Conus gloriamaris*). This particular cone shell was a real trophy still much prized today. His huge collection is in safe-keeping at The Natural History Museum, London.

The highest accolade must be to the sheer genius of the Swedish scientist Carolus Linnaeus or Karl von Linné (1707 - 1778) for the mammoth task of creating the binomial system or taxonomic classification. His binomial nomenclature is a system of classifying by a double name. The first being the name of the genus and the second that of the species within the genus, for example the Mediterranean Cone shell is *Conus mediterraneus*. This system provides a universal

Conus gloriamaris

understanding of plants and animals and though much modified, has stood the test of time. Linnaeus was ennobled for his work and is recognised in science as Linné or just L. Just as this internationally recognised formula prevents any doubt or misunderstanding over local variations, the name of the study of shells and molluscs, is universal too.

"Conchyliologie" and "malacologie" were introduced by French naturalists in the eighteenth century for this purpose. Today they translate as conchology and malacology, the former being the most recognised. Debated in the past as to which was the most proper, the favoured outcome seems to be that conchology is the study of molluscs and shells whereas malacology is the scientific study of molluscs. Conchology, I believe, is the older word and its definition makes greater sense as the shell is a product of the living mollusc, therefore it is almost impossible to regard one without the other.

LADIES PASTIMES

The eighteenth century also brought forth a great flurry of artistic exuberance when shells were fashionable and desirable for the decoration of anything from tiny boxes to ornate grottoes.

On the outskirts of the seaside town of Exmouth in Devon, overlooking the Exe estuary, sits A la Ronde known locally as The Round House. Built about 1795, on the instruction of two spinster cousins, the Misses Jane and Mary Parminter,

it was occupied as a family home until purchased by The National Trust in 1991. The many treasures within contain some exquisite examples of "shellery", culminating in an octagonal gallery with shell encrusted walls, created by Jane and Mary, gifted exponents of Victorian ladies amusements.

Pressed into a skin of lime putty, large chrysanthemums of limpets accompanied by contrasting chevrons of mussels adorn the window arches. Beneath a border of large cockles, another chevron formation of razor shells repeats a rhythmic pattern around an octagonal frieze, this same zigzag is echoed on the walls beneath the windows. Around and within this framework, a marvellous encrustation of shells, coloured glass, crystalline minerals, pebbles and pieces of broken china are worked. The final touch; little florets of lichen tucked into the putty, softening hard edges, filling all gaps and cleverly creating a suggestion of

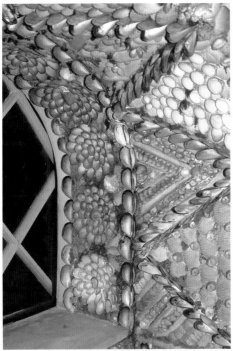

seaweed amongst the shells.

Today, a sturdy sycamore tree, left of the path from the car park to the barn at A la Ronde, is host to an abundance of the same lichen, while Exmouth beach still proves a fruitful source of cockles, mussels and razor shells. Could Jane and Mary have experienced the joy of harvesting materials from the "doorstep" as part of the greater pleasure in creating this unique testament to their skills?

Section of window arch, Shell Gallery.
A la Ronde

The elegant break-front cabinet in the Library reveals a collection of curios amassed by the cousins and displayed in true Victorian style, a real Cabinet of Curiosities. Inside, against a background of lively malachite green, is a delightful selection of prints, embellished with typical

Parminter chevron borders. The shelves below are crammed with tiny ornamental treasures- miniature boxes, alabaster fruits, bead necklaces, coral, crystals, minerals and shells,

Cabinet of Curiosities

a carved coconut shell, a flea catcher and more macabre, a squirrel's tail! A simple oblong tray with a centrepiece fashioned to resemble a daisy, has "petals" full of tiny shells, and is almost wedged into place by small, square "malachite" boxes, tightly set against one another and piled randomly with even more shells; overall, one great cacophony of scrumptious, full to the brim, organised chaos. The Drawing Room is also a paradise for shell lovers, from

the fireplace with its colourful jumble of shells to the more sophisticated shell pictures and flower dome, not forgetting "The Politician", sporting a natty suit of the tiniest mussel shells.

This room also contains an exceptional array of sand and seaweed pictures, a unique feather frieze and a large number of shells which once prompted a steward to pontificate to an attentive group of visitors:- quote. "Yes, yes, its suprising wot you can do dears wiv an 'andful of sand, some shells and a few fevvers!"

The Politician

31

A la Ronde is truly a most bewitching abode with much to offer; the outstanding diversity and range of its shells span the years from Victorian times to the present day illustrating the importance of their role in our lives.

A La Ronde set in surrounding meadowland

THE A LA RONDE COLLECTIONS

THE MELLOWS COLLECTION

Donated to The National Trust by Mrs Mellows of London, the collection remained in store at Hatchlands until 1991 when delivered to A la Ronde.

Initially, the shells were intended for repair to the Shell Gallery, but on unpacking were discovered to be a beautiful world-wide collection of marine and terrestrial shells wrapped in newspaper dated 1935, by coincidence the same year that A la Ronde opened its doors to visitors.

Within one box amongst the little newspaper parcels, was found a tiny mouse "fast asleep" in a perfect shredded nest. Christened "Samuel" he remained (under daily scrutiny) in a cabinet in the Sitting Room as part of a temporary display. He provided an amusing conversation piece for some time until Mother-Nature decided it was time for him to take a final bow!

In 1996 after the major task of cleaning and checking the classification of each shell, which occupied the best part of a year, a room on the upstairs corridor was decorated ready to receive the collection. More space than available was needed, so a rather battered chest of drawers on the ground floor was prepared to receive the snail shells.

Last year (2002), a fourth box of shells which evidently had been separated from the initial three, also found its way to A la Ronde necessitating a further winter's work to clean and classify. Once again, there were more shells than space and on this occasion a showcase on top of the chest of drawers was employed.

Below Stairs in the Showcase

Arranged formally in family groups, Cowrie shells peep out from shiny tubes and dishes, while a host of others look up from where they sit in their original blue cardboard trays and tiny glass topped boxes. Some rest on little cushions of cotton wool while the Ark shells (bivalves) are packed with the same and neatly tied to resemble their "inhabited look". A little card of Bulla shells traces the growth of young shells to adult and in another cabinet a row of Volute shells perch jauntily on a set of old cup hooks, while, beneath, three lovely fluted clams sit more elegantly on theirs.
The price of two shillings (sterling) on a large limpet shell

Clams

gives away secrets of age, while names and places beautifully inscribed in a variety of longhand styles create the aura of a long gone era. The collection is probably the combination of two or three smaller ones which have come together as a whole. The little cards and notes which accompany the shells are most fascinating adding another dimension with regard to the collectors.

Cowries and Bulla Shells

Without any provenance it is impossible to say who they were, however, several of these little missives when turned over, reveal themselves as calling cards with impressive names,

The Reverend A. R. Biddle of Farley Hill;
Lt. Col. Horace Walpole. Marlborough Club Heckfield Place;
Mr W. Mortimer Allfrey, Farley Castle, Junior Carlton Club;
The Reverend F. T. Lewarne;
Arthur Singleton Wynne;
Mr Shaddick Clode;
MR J. Friedlander ?;
Captain Cobham, Shinfield Manor.

Other scraps of paper used for classification are torn up wedding invitations. A jigsaw of these makes an almost complete version and reads as follows:-

Lady Russell requests the pleasure of
…. to the Wedding of her daughter
Cloé to The Hon Ernest Guinness
at St. Margarets, Westminster on
Wednesday July 15th at 1.15 and
afterwards at 14 Berkeley Square……
4.45

Maybe a further clue lies in the inscription on the back of a small pill-box lid containing a shell called Turbo vincten which reads, one pill to be taken a bedtime. G. Russell Esq. STAINET. Folkstone. 10/02/(18)83 ……….Who knows?

Missionaries on their far flung journeys became early collectors and a note enclosed with the following two cowries gives personal detail as well as classification.

2   *Cypraea tabescens   Solander?*
a. R.D. (Ceylon)
b. The younger & duller specimen belonged to my father' probably given him at Brighson ? about 1830 by Rev. J. Osborne an early Wesl. Missionary in Ceylon (whom I remember)
J.D.G.

Even more tantalising- is Brighson the name of a house and who was JDG?

Locations of shell finds are always an important accessory to the specimens, here, two more cowrie shells.
Cypraea
(one adult and one juvenile specimen)
from Panama Bay, entrance of the Canal Works.
Who would think that the entrance of a canal works would prove to be fruitful, when, on the face of things it seems an unlikely hunting spot.

The pencilled inscription on a razor shell
Picked up from the beach at the Golden Gate
                    San Francisco.
certainly raises the level of interest in a fairly plain shell turning it into an entertaining conversation piece.

This note included with a specimen of the Keyhole Limpet requires some concentration in reading but eventually the words fall into a rhythm (almost like modern rap) which renders it easier to understand.

Fissurella notwith the limpet shape assumed by its shell, is in affinity with the great cr...ed (crowned?) of spiral univalves. In an early stage it possesses a spiral shell, with a slit in the margin of the outer lip of the last whorl. As growth advances, shelly matter is deposited on both margins, which results in the slit becoming a whole and the spire a mere callosity until at last they coalesce in the apex of adult.

Below stairs in the showcase.

The oddballs of the Mellows Collection, most interesting, Sea Urchins, Chitons, Barnacles, Operculum, Ship Worm, and a grand selection of Snails.

The Goose Barnacle is the subject of a myth of peasant fisher folk in sixteenth century Europe who believed the stalked or ship barnacle was but a stage in the life of a goose-like bird, and that at certain seasons of the year the bird was formed within the barnacle shell, increasing in size, eventually making its escape into the water. The bird in question is rumoured to be the Brent Goose that

Stalked or Ship Barnacle

Referred to as
Goose
Barnacle.

winters upon our shores. The story, taken from Gerards Herbal 1597, tells how "the shells gape, the legs hang out,

that the bird growing bigger and bigger, the shells open
more and more, till at length it is attached only by the bill,
soon after which it drops into the sea; there it acquires
feathers and grows to a fowle".

Many shells and other treasures from the deep are found
by fishermen whilst gutting their catch, such as this
indigestible morsel.

*A barnacle cut from the belly of a whale caught in the Gulf
of Paria –
Trinidad   February 20th 1852.*

The coral reef provides another source of treasure and this next letter describes the growth of a mollusc, not as beautiful as some coral, but none the less quite a curiosity.

LOCKINGE HOUSE

WANTAGE   *Telegraph*

BERKS   *Ardington*

The Magilus Antiquus (Red Sea & Indian Ocean)

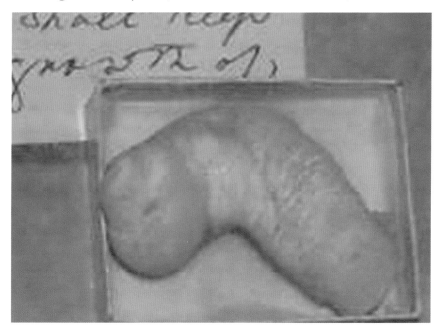

in the young form is shaped like a small Whelk. As the Coral to which it attaches itself increases in size the mollusc develops a long calcareous tube which it solidifies at the rear, while taking care that the aperture in front shall keep pace with the growth of the coral.

Spirula Peronii.

Spirula – *partly internal only a part of it being visible when on the animal.*

Puerto Oratava – Tenerife

allied to genus Sepia
separated whorls

<u>Spirula Squid (Spirula spirula) and shell.</u>

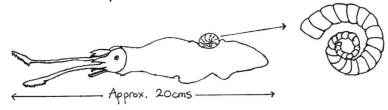

← Approx. 20cms →

The shell which protrudes slightly from the back of this squid-like decapod does not appear to serve any particular function. Unlike the shell, the squid is seldom found.

It is possible that the Spirula shell forms a buoyancy aid although this is unconfirmed

The Chest of Drawers,

This holds a myriad of snails from terrestrial and freshwater habitats revealing colours not usually associated with the snail; many have inspired shapes with incredible apertures like fancy key-holes.

The dreaded South African land snail resides at the back of the second shelf and is a monster in comparison to our own garden snail. Some time ago the Euglandina was introduced as an experiment to combat the problem of the destructive South African snail, which could massacre a garden in a very short time. The idea was that the carnivorous mollusc Euglandina would attack and eventually destroy enough of the South African snails to even the balance. However, the tables were turned when the Euglandina was overwhelmed by the sheer size of its quarry and proceeded to devour and eliminate many of the smaller species which were easier to digest.

More pleasantly, a story about the garden snail, Helix aspersa which shows the tenacity of the snail in its ability to hibernate for incredibly long periods, the longest known hibernation exceeds forty years. A Dublin merchant, Mr S. Simons inherited a collection of fossils, snails and curiosities from his father. Fifteen years later, his son was given the shells to play with, who placed them in a basin of water and much to his amazement several pairs of knobbed horns came into view !

Homer the Hermit Crab

Way down on the bottom shelf, at home with the Murex shells, is Homer the Hermit crab. Secured by a little hook on his tail inside his splendid residence he patiently waits for the children to come and find him.

THE SLATER COLLECTION

(Housed in The Butlers Pantry)

Set up in the winter of 1999/2000 the presentation here is based on the many guises of shells over the centuries from currency and bartering, art and architecture, religion and mythology, craft and decoration, to commerce and collection. In the far corner is an old plate rack, now co-opted to be a display case with a selection of cone shells on the top shelf.

These beautifully coloured intricately patterned shells are prized by collectors. The molluscs are carnivorous and stun their prey with a self renewing poison barb. Some are more virulent than others with five species known to be capable of a fatal sting. The Tulip cone is the most venomous, however, the Geography cone has been responsible for more deaths. Wearing only a net slung around the waist in which to carry live cones to the surface, many native divers have succumbed to the wrath of an angry mollusc.

Amongst a scattering of small cowries and a tangle of seaweed there are plenty of other collectors' favourites, of which the Golden Cowrie, also known as Morning Dawn or Orange Cowrie is the main attraction. This individual shell is held in high esteem by the South West Pacific islanders who wear it as a mark of distinction.

Nocturnal friends the Olives, are strewn on another shelf dwarfed by Chambered Nautilus and three very large shells,

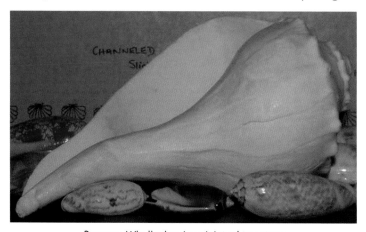

Busycon Whelk showing sinistral aperture

a Busycon Whelk (☺sinistral), a Giant Philippine Cockle and the uncommon Giant Tun.

Popular for their beautifully sculpted and elegant exteriors, a bevy of scallops, clams, oysters, murex and tibia grace another shelf.

The massive proportions of the Baler shells, which are obviously named because of their functional and ergonomic shape, fulfil the duties of carrying and emptying water more prettily than a bucket.

☺ left handed aperture.

Neighbour to these and also a water carrier more on the lines of a watering can, is the False Trumpet of "jumbo" proportions, accredited to be the largest gastropod (snail) in the world, giving rise to the thought, "exactly how large was the inhabitant?" Above sits the musical section. Two trumpets, the Sacred Chank, associated with weddings, warfare and ceremonial "trumpetings" and the most beautifully patterned Trumpet shell (Triton) used from Neolithic times. Adapted by sawing off the tip or boring a hole in the side, its strains once echoed throughout the Mediterranean. A small industry once thrived around the romantically named Silkworm of the Sea or as it is properly known the Noble Pen shell. Byssus threads secreted by a special gland in the mollusc's foot produce silky, golden bronze strands as fine as hair. It was possible to spin the yarn into garments which looked so dainty and yet were so strong they were virtually indestructible. A pair of ladies gloves would fold minutely enough to fit into an empty walnut shell.

Jewellery springs to mind as the final touch befitting such apparel. Often referred to as "jewels of the sea" the Abalones, Ear shells and Ormers provide rainbow coloured mother of pearl or silver nacre for such trinkets.

The Pearl Oyster makes a perfect pearl after the invasion of a foreign particle, such as a grain of sand, which it is unable to flush out. Natural pearl building cells multiply around the intruder until it is covered with pearl.

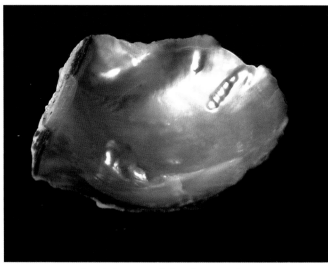

Pearl Oyster with Pearl formations

The classic cameo, worn mostly as a brooch is made from the warmly contrasting orange and brown colours of the Bullmouth Helmet shell. Cameo cutters carve in relief out of the top layer and cut away surrounding parts to reveal contrasting backgrounds. They are still produced in

Italy and Florida which have always been famous for the intricacy of their engravings.

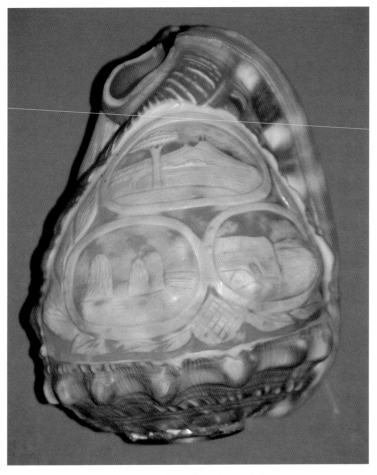

Carved Bullmouth Helmet Shell

Turban and Top shells hunted relentlessly by divers between 1918 and 1939 for the manufacture of buttons were saved, fortunately, by the growth of the plastics industry.

The rich and regal purple is sourced from the Purple Dye Murex. The colourless liquid collected from the molluscs' dye gland undergoes several changes of colour when exposed to light, finally achieving the colour purple. Termed "Royal" or "Tyrian" purple, it was used for colouring royal robes, and later for tinting the lips and cheeks of Roman ladies. The Dog Whelk also produces a dye lighter than the murex which was used throughout the British Isles for staining parchment, setting off gold and silver lettering and, more mundanely, by crofters to dye their homespun tweeds.

Sea Urchins

The Sea Urchin like the Sand Dollar belongs to a group of creatures called Echinoderms who dwell at the bottom of the sea. The shell, or "test" was once used as a trendy enhancement for the light bulb, its warm coral pink, purple and orange glowed from many an alcove or dark corner.

The Scallop is probably the most well known of all, predominantly featured in art and architecture, beloved as The Pilgrim scallop, emblem of St. James the Apostle (St. James of Compostella) patron saint of pilgrims and worn as a badge, attached to the wide brim of a hat, satchel or staff as protection against the devil and his fiends.

The Venus Flower Basket

A rare treat, nestling amidst a variety of corals under the watchful eye of a large starfish or two is the fragile looking structure of a sponge (phylum porifera). The Venus Flower Basket, so named for the intricate lacework of its silicious spicules, grows in the deep water off The Philippines. The sponge was once thought to be a plant however, closer research has shown it to be an active animal. Food is filtered out and eaten from water pumped through the small opening and out through the larger ones. This flimsy looking structure must filter one ton of water in order to gain an ounce in body weight.

THE CHEEK COLLECTION 2001

During his career with The Royal Air Force, Eddie Cheek worked as an Air Traffic Controller in East Africa (Mombassa & Zanzibar) in 1964, and as Comptroller of Post and Telecommunications -Director of Aviation- in the Pacific (Solomon Islands) from 1967 to 1977.

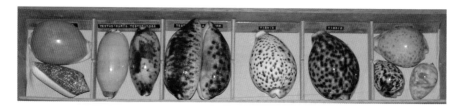

Part of Eddie's collection of Cowries showing his specimens of The Golden Cowrie & The Glory of the Sea (above left)

A keen amateur shell collector, he put together this fine collection of Cowrie, Cone and Volute shells which are meticulously classified and inventoried.

He must have been overjoyed to achieve two of the most prized specimens, the Golden Cowrie and the Glory of the Sea (cone shell). A press cutting accompanies the cone shell, which relates to the discovery of this particular one amongst a box of discarded shells- just imagine the thrill! The National Trust is very grateful to his wife and family who donated the collection in his memory for education and research in the field of conchology. It is available for study by prior arrangement.

THE ROGERS COLLECTION 2002

A good "all round" collection with a wonderful range and variety of specimens from the large and glamorous to the small and appealing, some displayed in black, glass-topped boxes, others loose. At the time of receiving this donation,

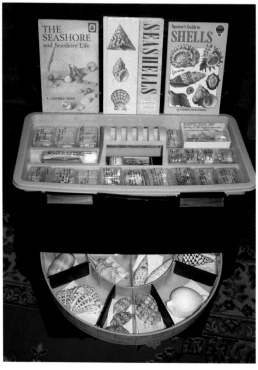

from Mrs Rogers of Brighton, ideas regarding a "handling collection" had been mooted without conclusion; however, fate must have taken a hand because it fitted the bill perfectly.

For practical purposes it is kept in a large tool box which can be wheeled or carried. It has the handy facility of breaking down into several smaller containers and adapts perfectly with its great variety of compartments. Large shells are encased in bubble-wrap envelopes with basic details of type and location attached, smaller specimens in clear tubes or boxes are labelled with interesting snippets; the inclusion of three books completes a very easy-going, portable collection.

THE DOME OF CONCHOLOGY 2003

A hotchpotch of shells, fossils, corals, tiny sea urchins, baby starfish, minute shells, beads and little glass containers holding lucky beans all tossed into a grand dome shaped jar. A blackbirds face, hand painted on the jawbone of a fish, smirks knowingly through the glass. This lovely rounded, shiny jar full of "goodies" brightens a dark corner in the Entrance Hall at A la Ronde. Passed on by Paulene Cullen (now retired) of Paulene's

Hat Shop in Budleigh Salterton, who acquired them as part of a job lot at auction.

MY "AMUSEMENTS"

Whether a Victorian lady or a twenty-first century girl the pleasures of collecting and decorating with shells are as great now as they were two hundred years ago.

The shipping of shells, as ballast, probably no longer occurs, but happily there is a retail trade still supplying those enchanting little pink and pearly shells coveted by ladies of leisure. Finding your own is much more fun and I often wonder, when happily on hands and knees in the sand, nose to the ground, whether our Victorian counterparts foraged in this way.

There is an anecdote which demonstrates this pastime was not only confined to the fairer sex. About 1850, Mr Batchelor of Buckie House, Anstruther, Scotland, decorated the front and halfway up the side of his house with shells or "buckies", as they are called in Fife. He also decorated the ceiling of a room inside the house which became known as the grotto. The enterprising Mr B. charged visitors who wished to view the grotto, which incidentally housed his coffin, also covered with buckies and for a further remuneration he would obligingly climb inside and shut the lid!

My own shell gathering has afforded me many happy hours with my children who loved to forage too. They soon became experts at finding the best shells and our expeditions throughout summer and winter provided a huge "stash".

One day we gazed into a shop window at a clown made of limpet shells. He was cleverly assembled with limpets piledone on top of another and decorated with bright yellow and brown periwinkles. His feet were two lovely big blue/black mussels, and if I remember correctly, he had a

"shell hoop" slung carelessly over one arm.

From that moment collecting became creative and almost compulsive. Homeward to raid our precious hoard of shells and try my hand at a likeness. Inspired by a modicum of success, shell ladies came next, followed by frogs then little sailing ships.

Since those days I have become more adventurous and love to mosaic little table tops and other small pieces of furniture with shells but boxes are my real favourites.

I particularly enjoy decorating the underside of a lid to create an element of surprise; the box keeping its secret till the lid is lifted, shells pristine!

Having scoured the beach for shells, I browse in the charity shops and recycling centres which are good hunting grounds for bric-a-brac to mosaic, and a pound or two will purchase a suitable bargain.

Making the start on a new acquisition can be rather daunting, the blank space like an empty page, waits for some

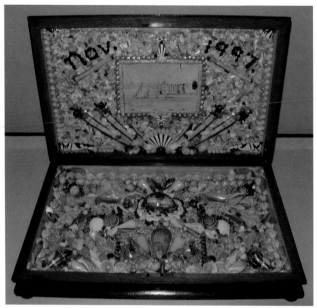

inkling; some pearl not fully clear as yet in "the minds eye". Some will map out a precise pattern and rigidly adhere to it, but I favour the casual approach. I shuffle and muddle shapes and colours until an acceptable pattern emerges, then, like "Topsy" it just grows!

Naturally interlocking and evocative of their own style and rhythm, it is the shells themselves which produce the inspiration. As for colours anything goes; orange, pink and purple shells snuggle together and blend as happily as flowers in a bed – nothing could be simpler or more satisfying...................................My Cornucopia.

GLOSSARY

Acetic Acid A clear or liquid acid that gives vinegar its characteristic taste.

Binomial Nomenclature The system of classifying by a double name e.g. Mediterranean cone- Conus mediterraneus.

Bivalvia Bi-valves, shells with two hinged parts e.g. clams, mussels and oysters

Bynes Disease A chemical reaction which attacks a shell.

Byssus threads Silky threads discharged by a mussel in order to secure itself usually to a rock or pier.

Calcium Acetate Formate compound salt.

Cephalopoda Having a beaked head or an internal shell (cuttlefish) and prehensile tentacles e.g. squids, octopus and chambered nautilus.

Conchology The study of molluscs and shells.

Decapod A mollusc such as a squid or cuttlefish with ten arm like tentacles. This can also refer to crustaceans such as the crab, lobster or shrimp with five pairs of legs.

Echinoderms Marine invertebrates including starfish, sea urchins and sea cucumbers, the body often prickly or covered with spines.

Efflorescence Surface salt crystallization.

Formic Acid A colourless irritant and volatile acid (also produced by ants).

Gastropoda Snails and Slugs.

Genera Classes having common characteristics

Hygroscopic To attract water.

Hypostracum The (Aragonite) inner layer of a shell.

Invertebrate An animal without backbone or spinal column.

Laminaria (Oar Weed) A type of seaweed with root like structures called holdfasts which provide the plant with an anchor similar to tree roots in soil. They do not absorb nutrients but provide shelter on the shore and habitat for many small animals within their forests.

Malacology The scientific study of molluscs.

Mollusc A soft bodied animal belonging to the Phylum Mollusca.

Monoplacophora (Gastroverms) Rare and primitive molluscs related to ancestors from about four hundred million years ago in the Devonian Period. Tiny, thin limpet like shells with a little sloping point rather like a pixie hood.

Operculum The horny, limy disc which secures the aperture of a shell.

Ostracum The (Calcium Carbonate) middle layer of a shell.

Periostracum The (Conchiolin) outer layer of a shell.

Phylum Mollusca A major primary division of the animal kingdom made up of classes of soft bodied, unsegmented animals usually having a hard shell.

Phylum Porifera The division of the animal kingdom designated to the "pore bearers" or sponges so called for their possession of millions of pores.

Polyplacophora Chitons, sometimes called Sea Cradles. The shells consist of eight overlapping transverse plates and resemble garden wood lice.

Provenance A known origin

Scaphopoda Tusk shells or tooth shells, tube like and shaped like a tusk.

Silicious Consisting of silica (flint or limestone).

Sinistral Pertaining to a gastropod shell that has its aperture to the left when facing the observer with the tip or apex held upwards. The Lightning Whelk, Busycon contrarium Conrad, is the exception as it is naturally sinistral.

Spicule A small needle like structure.

AND JUST FOR FUN
CONSTRUCT A "CLIVE"

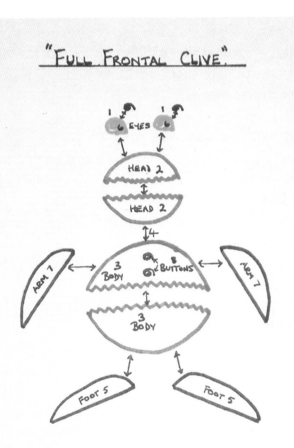

"FULL FRONTAL CLIVE"

You will need:

1 tube clear p.v.a. adhesive.

1 small pot of black modelling paint.

1 fine paintbrush.

WHAT TO DO.

Read carefully before starting!!
Visit the beach and collect two pairs of mussels (not too large), one large pair of cockles, one smaller pair of cockles, two matching yellow flat winkles and two or three minute flat winkles or something similar for buttons. Make sure all "body parts" are in proportion. Clean and dry thoroughly and you are ready to start.

1. Using black modelling paint prepare eyes by painting two black "tadpoles" on the curly centre part of the yellow flat winkles, until the eyes look back at you!!!!!! (Allow to dry).
2. Glue both edges of the pair of small cockles (the head) together.
3. Glue both edges of the pair of large cockles (the body)together.
4. When dry, fix head to the body, hold or prop the two parts together until the glue sets.
5. Arrange the feet (pair of mussels) into a suitable standing position. Take the joined head and body and balance them on top of the feet until they sit comfortably without toppling over, then glue.
6. Arrange eyes (yellow flat winkles) on top of head,and glue.
7. Hold arms (pair of mussels) against the sides of the body, when you are happy with their position, glue.
8. Lastly, stick two or three minute shell buttons on his chest.

BIBLIOGRAPHY

Beautiful Shells
H. G. Adams   **1871**

Compendium of Seashells
R. Tucker Abbott & S. Peter Dance   **1982**
(ISBN 0 525 93269 0)

Denizens of the Deep
F. Martin Duncan   **1917**

Heritage Illustrated Dictionary of the English Language
William Morris (Ed)   **1973**
(ISBN 07 00 11 73 7)

Regency and Victorian Crafts
Jane Toller   **1969**

Shell Life
Edward Step   **1901**

Shells
Mary Saul   **1975**
(ISBN 0 600 380483)

Shells of Britain and Europe
Jan Lellak   **1975**
(ISBN 0 600 380203)

The Naturalist at the Seashore (Peeps at Nature)
Richard Elmhirst   **1913**

RECOMMENDED READING

Younger Readers

Eyewitness Explorers-Shells   1993
(ISBN 07513-60031)
Junior Nature Guides Seashells   1993
(ISBN 1 85028 218 8)

Pocket Sized

The Green Guide Seashore Life of Britain & Europe.
1996
Bob Gibbons
(ISBN 1 85368 172 5)
Letts Pocket Guide to Seashells   1991
Eleanor Lawrence & Sue Harniess
(ISBN 1 85238 114 0)

Reference Books

Compendium of Seashells   1982
R. Tucker Abbott & S. Peter Dance
(ISBN 0 525 93269 0)
Seashells of the World   1981
Jerome M. Eisemberg
(ISBN 1 870630 74 2)
Seashells of the Northern Hemisphere   1991
R. Tucker Abbott
(ISBN 1 85028 113 0)
Shells Treasures from the Sea   1979
James A. Cox
(ISBN 0 7112 0011 4)
Sowerbys' Book of Shells
A re-issue of The Conchological Manual of 1852
ISBN 1 85170 440X   1990

..............trimmed with feathers from the A la Ronde Guinea Fowl flock

Notes